GOD's *extraordinary* LOVE

Title: **God's Extraordinary Love**

Various contributors
Editor & Composer: Kathy Watson Swift
Copyright © 2024

An initiative of The Church of God We Women of Excellence
www.wewomenofexcellence.com

Designed & Published by: Galilee.com
www.galilee.com

Royal Library reg.nr: 020-14249
ISBN: 978-94-93105-23-2

Introduction

Scan the QR code or visit the following link:

https://youtu.be/BDgvUP2uQfs

Dedication

God's extraordinary love is dedicated to the many outstanding women across our 13 countries and three islands of Western Europe. Countless seeds of love have been sown in many hearts by our outstanding women's leadership in the Church of God. Women everywhere have realized that they are vessels of purpose, loved, ordained and commissioned by God himself to show forth his love at work in their everyday lives!

Each devotion shares an intimate story, life experience or intimate thought that will encourage your heart and renew a fresh outlook on life. God's extraordinary love is right there beside you and it is meant for you.

I want to thank my husband, Chris, who encouraged me to pursue what God put in my heart for our women.

As well as Rev. John & Shakila Olsen for their relentless hours spent designing and putting our first devotional book together. Without them and each lady who participated, nothing could have been accomplished.

Thank you for helping share God's love with others by purchasing this E-book. This book is uniquely designed to reach women in as many as five different languages.

Connect with us with a review at:
wewomenofexcellence.com

Paula

HILL

Paula Hill is the wife of Timothy M. Hill, General Overseer for the Church of God, Cleveland, Tennessee. They have three daughters, Melinda, Brittany, and Tara, and five grandchildren, Timothy Brayden, Hailey Taylor, Lucas Reid Maness, Jaxon River and Jameson Hill Sharpe. Paula currently serves as the International Women's Director for Church of God Women's Ministries.

She previously served as the World Missions Coordinator for Church of God World Missions and has served on the Church of God Women's Ministries Advisory Committee since 2004. She has also served as a keynote speaker for many conventions, camp meetings, and conferences.

We are living in a time when everyone seems to be trying to reinvent themselves. This seems especially true as we are slowly emerging from the two-year "pandemic" that has resulted in great loss and agonizing grief for so many. We feel compelled to fit into the culture and be "relevant." If we don't dress the part or use the right words, we don't seem to belong to the "in" crowd.

Sadly, these attitudes have crept into the church. We compare our gifts and anointing to others, and as a result, we often fall short in our own eyes. Just as many of you, I confess that I have struggled with these feelings in my own life. Over the last few years God has dealt very strongly with me on these insecurities. These feelings bring fear and anxiety and the perception of being on the outside of relevance and looking in. I am now convinced that the fear of failure often comes because we try to function outside of what Christ has called us to be.

Recently, I have been deeply moved by the Holy Spirit, and stirred by a particular passage of scripture. It is highlighted and underlined in every Bible I have, and now serves as a constant reminder to me:

"So, since we find ourselves fashioned into all these excellently formed and marvelously functioning parts in Christ's body, let's just go ahead and be what we were made to be, without enviously or pridefully comparing ourselves with each other, or trying to be something we aren't."

Romans 12:5-6 (Message)

Nothing is unimportant if it is what God has called me to do!

*Whatever part of the body you represent is a piece of
the puzzle that shows God's personality to the world.
It paints a small section of the picture of who God is.
So, if you have the gift of compassion,
that's a very important piece of who God is.
If you are an encourager, that's who God is.*

If you are a teacher, that's who God is.
If you are a speaker or have a preaching ministry,
that's who God is.
If you are a stay-at-home Mom, as I was,
you are given an awesome opportunity to show
many facets of who God is to your children.

All these pieces complete the puzzle, but sometimes, it is a difficult decision to just be yourself. Theodore Roosevelt said, *"Comparison is the thief of joy."*

I want to function and serve faithfully in the role my Father has called me to. I've offered myself as a living sacrifice to His service. We can't question why He chose us to be the part of the body we are. He knows where He needs us, so we should determine to give that our all. You are valuable to the Lord who has called you to excel in your assignment for Him. Remember, if you are the missing piece, the puzzle is incomplete. Even the edge pieces are vital and necessary to complete the picture.

Prayer:

"God, please place me where You want me and
need me to be. I know I'm a valuable part of the
body of Christ and am an important part of who
You are. Thank You for using me."

Amen.

Paula Hill

LOVE NEVER GIVES UP,

NEVER LOSES FAITH, AND

endures

THROUGH EVERY CIRCUMSTANCE.

{1 CORINTHIANS 13:7}

# *Janice*

PARK

Janice is a Pastor serving in Ireland alongside her husband Nick Park, who is the National Overseer of the Church of God. She is a gifted musician and songwriter who loves to lead others in worship. She is presently working towards a Bachelor's degree in Psychotherapy.

God's love is so powerful! It is so great to know about the love of God as well as to read about the love of God, but the most powerful thing is when you experience the love of God yourself. When you see the love of God in an answer to prayer. It is in those times when you have cried out to

God. He came and made His presence known in a very real way.

There was a particular time in my life when I probably needed God more than ever before. This was the time when my daughter, Grace died. She was just four years old.

Grace was born weighing only 2lb 15oz (1.3kg). It was discovered a few months later, after she couldn't feed properly, that she had a condition called Familial Dysautonomia. She had to be fed by a tube all her life. The automatic functions in her body didn't work properly and she was eventually permanently put on oxygen.

We were continually praying for God to heal her but she died on our wedding anniversary. The words on her gravestone we had inscribed were "Safe with her Lord."

Amidst this great devastation, heartbreak, grief and loss, there was a sense within us that her suffering was truly over. She was safe with her Lord, who she had asked into her life. Grace often lifted her hands in praise to her favorite song, "The Lord reigns." One day we will be reunited with her, in the safety and presence of our Eternal loving Father God, singing 'The Lord reigns.'

This was a very deep, dark time, when I cried out for the Lord. I needed His presence, I needed His comfort, and I needed His love. Somebody gave me a poem, which was just right for me in that season. It was the poem "Footprints."

This poem is a powerful illustration of the extraordinary love of God. He is always with us. He will never leave us or forsake us. Even in times when it feels dark, lonely, barren and desolate in our lives, (when we think He has abandoned us), He is actually there all the time, walking with us in our pain, and even carrying us.

The greatest lesson I realized in this, is that sometimes when we feel that the most important thing in our life is what we do for God, or accomplish for God, this is not it! But when you have loss in your life, and you are in that broken hurting place, there is nothing you can do for God. There is so much that God will do for you. These are times when we need to allow Him to minister to us, to carry us.

The poem is all about such situations. In my life, when I couldn't put one foot in front of the other, when I was so overtaken with grief with a sense of loss and sadness, that was the time and the season that His love carried me. There was only one set of footprints in that desolate desert of my life, because God carried me. He didn't only carry me through that grief but sustained me.

A few months after Grace died, I remember going to the beach beside a harbor and looking out to sea. I felt like I had been a ship sailing happily out at sea serving God, but here I was now in the harbor. I was like a broken boat, damaged from the storms at sea and in need of repair. I wondered if I could ever sail happily again. I felt lost and empty. It is that feeling one gets when there is a loss of a loved one.

A time of emptiness. A loss from one's sense of meaning and purpose in life. All hope had been crushed, and faith is at its lowest. I felt vulnerable. My trust in God was a bit shaky, because I had prayed believing for healing, but now Grace was no longer with me. I had been out in the storms of life. I had been tossed around and bashed, now lay broken and wounded in the harbor.

How many times have we been in that wounded broken place, saying to God, "What can I do? What use am I? How can you use me, God? I've been out there at sea, I've given it my best, I've tried to serve you Lord but here I am in the harbor, a broken boat full of holes. If I tried to go out to sea, I know I would sink immediately."

That was the cry of my soul as I looked out upon that vast sea. But God met with me there and He spoke into my broken wounded soul.

He said to me, "How much trust do you have?" I pinched my thumb and finger together, and held them up to God, indicating that there was very little.

God said, "Give me what you have. I will take it and multiply it. You will sail the sea again. You will be powerful in ministry for me."

In my broken place, I could not yet see or envision that ever happening, but I did what he asked. I gave that little bit of trust to God, believing that He was taking care of me. I did sail the sea again. I did smile again. I did and I am still doing powerful ministry. I allow God to pour His extraordinary love into and through me to touch others. I am fulfilled, flourishing and daily overwhelmed by His love, grace, mercy and gifts that are lavished on me.

The harbor of our lives at times seems like the place of rejection, abandonment, brokenness and failure, but it is in fact our refuge. It is the safe place to go, the place of God's appointing and anointing, a harbor of love. It is the place of strength, empowering, and renewing. It can be likened to the cleft of the rock where God shields us, and where we find shelter from the storm.

We all need a harbor to go to. It is the harbor of God's extraordinary love, where He gently takes what feels broken, battered, useless, tossed aside, unfit for service, finished, hopeless, and worthless. He then begins to repair the damage. He will pour in healing love, bring restoration, and launch us once again as a beautiful vessel fit for service.

My prayer for you is:

Ask him for his help and his love will be poured out for you just as he did for me. He is waiting for you today.

Janice Park

Footprints

One night a man had a dream. He dreamed he was walking along the beach with the Lord. Across the sky flashed scenes from his life. For each scene, he noticed two sets of footprints in the sand; one belonged to him, and the other to the Lord.

When the last scene of his life flashed before him, he looked back at the footprints in the sand. He noticed that many times along the path of his life there was only one set of footprints. He also noticed that it happened at the very lowest and saddest times in his life.

This really bothered him, and he questioned the Lord about it. "Lord, you said that once I decided to follow you, you'd walk with me all the way. But I have noticed that during the most troublesome times in my life, there is only one set of footprints. I don't understand why when I needed you most you would leave me."

The Lord replied, "My precious, precious child, I love you and I would never leave you. During your times of trial and suffering, when you see only one set of footprints, it was then that I carried you."

Krystal
Bono

The Love of God

Krystal is the wife of Reverend Sal Bono and mother to Emma, Sophia, Olivia and Nora. She is an ordained minister, singer, speaker and currently serves as the Spiritual Life Pastor of a large Foursquare Christian School in Charlotte, N. C. Her passion is to finish her Ministry Leadership degree by July 2023 which will assist her in helping ministry families be whole and healed while serving others.

The Love of God has taken a chance on me continuously throughout my life. As a wife and mother now at the age of 42 there are many times I can look back on my life and see how the love of Christ carried me. At the age of 8, I can remember being at church camp in Southern Illinois in the United States. This was my first-time attending camp on my own.

I was going into 3rd grade, and I was so excited to have this experience. After the evening service, there was an alter call and several of those in my cabin went down to receive the Holy Spirit, with evidence of speaking in other tongues. Even now as I think of this, it continues to be a life changing moment in my spiritual walk. Because it was in that moment, I felt the presence of God in a very real way. This was a new experience for me. Growing up in church and as a pastor's kid, I had been in a lot of church services. This, however, was a first for me.

I will never forget that experience as one of God's outpourings of love in my life. Fast forward to now over thirty years later and I cannot even begin to count the endless sea of expressions of God's love. After losing my father to cancer at the age of 10, God showed his love to me through dreams of myself walking hand in hand with my dad in Heaven.

The Father always gives our hearts what we need, because he understands us and created us in his image. Often, I think we forget that the Father gave us His only son so that we could walk in communion with Him. This scripture found in John 3:16 is one that is foundational to our relationship with God and his love for us. How Faithful is the father to us to show us the depth of love through His own sacrifice.

I find it so true that in our lives as we give ourselves fully to Christ, that we are as well pouring out as a drink offering to the one who fills us up. Ladies, let me encourage you today, wherever you find yourself.

My prayer for you:

Remember God Loves you, that He sees you and that He has felt everything you are feeling. Step out and ask God to meet you and know that God's faithfulness and His love will never fail you. Be Strong and Courageous dear one. The Love of Christ flows and meets you now wherever you are. Walking with you in this journey of faith.

Krystal Bono

"…He has given us the *Holy Spirit* to fill our hearts with His love."

—Romans 5:5

Sharon

TUITE

God's Extraordinary Love

Sharon is a member of the worship team in the Solid Rock Church Drogheda, Ireland and has a BA (Hon.) degree in Youth Work. She works in Oberstown Children's Detention Campus for young offenders. She is passionate about working with youth and children as well as sharing God's love. Her hobbies are photography, art and music.

When I think about God's love it brings me back to last year. During this time in work my manager began to humiliate and bully the team I worked with. This went on for three months. The situation ended up going to senior management and the Human resource office. Through the process of mediation between the team and my manager, a lot of hurt and disappointment was expressed from both perspectives. To some extent there was a resolution agreed on.

Then, later that same year I was involved in two horrific incidents with the young people I work with. The incidents left me unable to work, and I was out on injury leave for five months. During these five months I was seen by Doctors and Specialists, had x-rays, scans, and medication, as well as talked with an occupational therapist. It was a very hard time.

While I was off work, I questioned God. I wondered where he was, and if I would ever play in the worship team again? I was also concerned if I ever would get back to the job that I loved. It was my job that God had opened the door for me to have.

With all I had left within me I picked up the guitar and started to worship God. I sang about how grateful I was for all He had brought me through. I sang about how He would bring me through and out of this mess that I was going through.

I sat, I cried, I waited, I listened, and through all of my worship, God repeatedly said to me, no matter how I felt, He loved me. I continued to worship, to seek and to question. He continued to remind me, "He loved me and would never leave me. Was I not listening to him? Was I so used to moaning and being in a self-pity mode?" To be honest, I think he got tired of me playing the same record. The record would have been an extended version called 'locked in self-pity with no one to blame'. If it was a book, it could be called '50 ways to bury yourself in self-pity'.

Thank God he doesn't get tired of hearing us and he truly listens. I kept seeking and asking, then one night while I was praying in the midst of my tears, God came down from a mountain and reached out his hand to me at that moment. I could feel God's love. I knew He cared.

God took time out for Me. I realized he loved me no matter how I was feeling, no matter what my level of anxiety or pain was. His love will never change, and in my darkest of moments, his love will never fail me and never will his love leave me.

His great love is for all of us. Regardless of where you are, he is listening.

"Draw nigh to God and He will draw nigh unto you."
James 4:8

Sharon Tuite

FOR WE LIVE BY

faith,

NOT BY SIGHT.
- 2 CORINTHIANS 5:7 -

Chris
KETTLE

Sunshine on my balcony

I am Chris Kettle, wife of Graham Kettle, the National Overseer of Luxembourg. I am a member of Oasis Church of God Luxembourg and function as the Missions Coordinator. We have 3 daughters and 3 granddaughters living in the UK and 1 grandson living in the US. We also have 2 dogs, one recently adopted from a shelter in Malta. We have recently taken Luxembourgish nationality. I love to share in the many activities of my local church such as women's ministry and serve in the church's missions.

I have just come in from sitting on the balcony in my back garden. For those of you who live in Southern Europe, with all your lovely sunshine, I know you are thinking so what! But here in Luxembourg it is very unusual to have such lovely sunshine in March, especially as this morning there was frost on the ground.

God's creation never fails to move me. God made all this in seven days, and yet here we are centuries later His creation is still perfect, the trees may lose their leaves in Autumn but they grow beautiful and green in the season of Spring. The Forsythia bush outside my kitchen window already has buds on it, soon it will have beautiful yellow flowers reminding me of new life. I find my walk with God is rather like His creation, I hear His word and even though I have been a Christian for many years, I hear and see something new, His word becomes new and fresh like the spring each year. The difference is that His word does not die like the leaves in the Autumn and Winter. His word is also a bit like the daffodils, the bulbs are in the ground seemingly hidden but then as the weather warms up they come to life.

When we read God's word, maybe the secret is hidden but as we read and trust God, His word comes to life. I find this song such a blessing, it is not a new song but God's word never fades;

*The steadfast love of the Lord never ceases, His mercies never come
to an end, They are new every morning New every morning,
Great is Thy faithfulness, O Lord Great is Thy faithfulness,*

It is taken from Lamentations 3:22 & 23. The writer has been having a hard time. Maybe that is you today, with all that is going on in the world at the moment, we are in worrying times but as the final verse of Lamentations 3 says:

*I say to myself, "The Lord is my portion;
therefore I will wait for Him."*

Chris Kettle

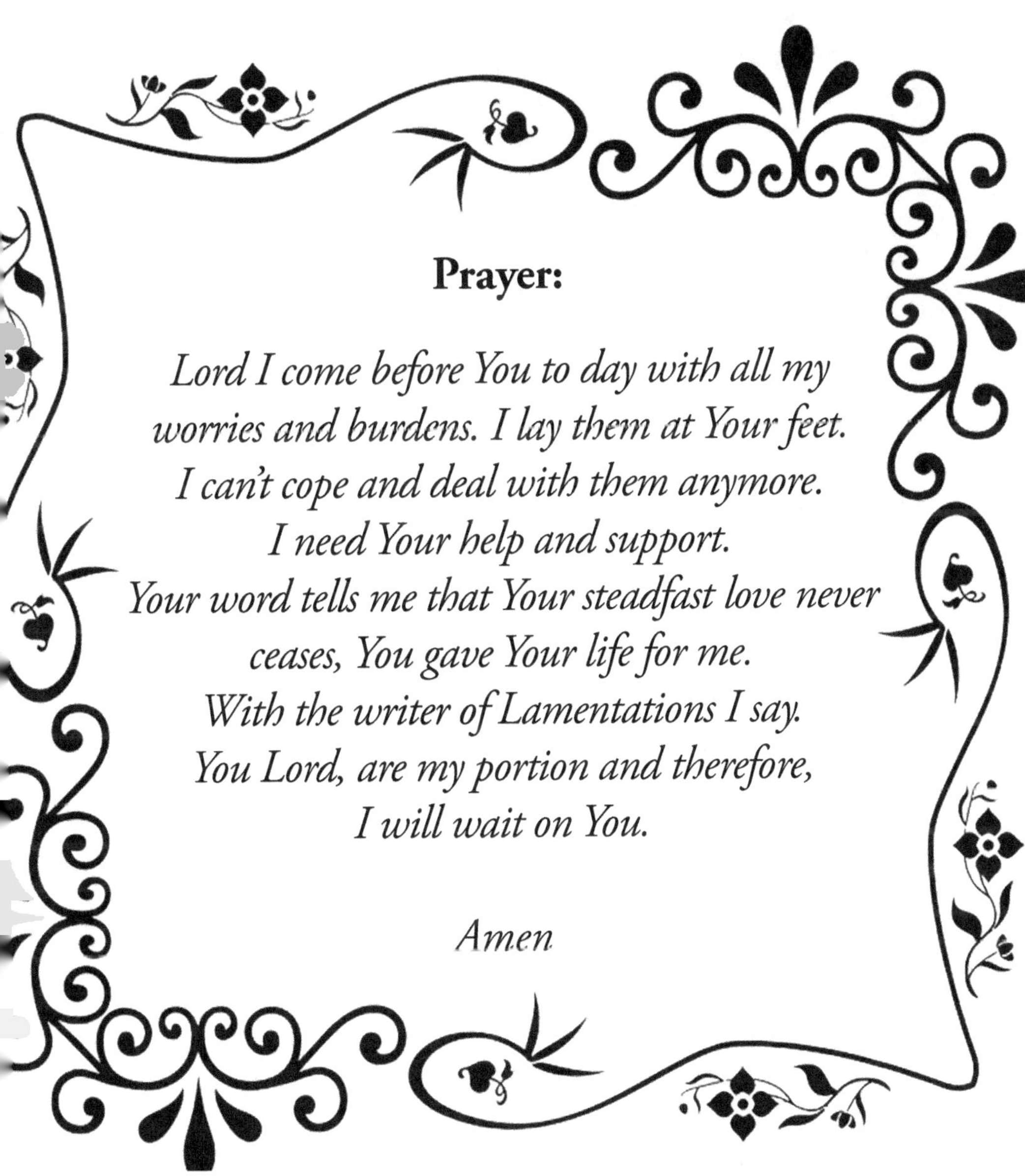

Prayer:

*Lord I come before You to day with all my
worries and burdens. I lay them at Your feet.
I can't cope and deal with them anymore.
I need Your help and support.
Your word tells me that Your steadfast love never
ceases, You gave Your life for me.
With the writer of Lamentations I say.
You Lord, are my portion and therefore,
I will wait on You.*

Amen

Yen

TAN

Tested by Covid

Yen Tan is married to Terence Tan. She and her husband are members of the Oasis Church of God in Luxembourg where she serves with joy in the Women's Fellowship. They have a daughter who is currently studying in the UK.

The pandemic has brought me "the best of times and the worst of times." This is my testimony of God's extraordinary miraculous love.

I had flown solo back to Singapore in the midst of very stringent Covid restrictions. A two-week quarantine was mandatory for all arriving travellers, so we boarded buses from the airport destined for different hotels. We had no choice or knowledge of which hotel we would be going to. I thought I will be happy whatever hotel, but the verse, "You do not have because you do not ask God" (James 4:2) suddenly popped into my head.

So I prayed jokingly, "How about the Ritz-Carlton, Lord?" As the bus arrived at our destination, some passengers started gesturing excitedly. Yes, I saw that we were indeed at the Ritz- Carlton, a renown 5-star hotel! When I saw my luxurious room, with its spectacular city view, I could not stop thanking God for His goodness and his love!

On the third day, while enjoying my 'personal retreat', I carried out a required Antigen Rapid Test (ART). My eyes stared, bewildered to see the positive result. I did not have any symptoms but a false positive test was extremely low.

I was instructed to pack an overnight bag and an ambulance immediately whisked me off to a Covid facility where they performed a more conclusive PCR test. If it was positive, I would be transported to hospital the following day. If negative, I would be required to stay an extra day for a second PCR test.

I asked the doctor regarding the probability of a false positive ART; he confirmed that the likelihood was very small. My mind despaired of the potential outcome. "What's happening, Lord?"

I was then taken to another hotel, a basic room with a sea- view. Thoughts of having Covid and needing to be hospitalized brought me to my knees in prayer. I finally told God I would accept His will cheerfully and surrendered everything to him.

I did not sleep well, tossing and turning. I awoke suddenly in the early hours to hear Jesus' words, "If you have faith, you can say to this mountain, 'Move', and it will move." (Matthew 17:20).

I responded, "Lord, I have faith in You." So I began to cast my 'Covid Mountain' into the nearby sea and prayed that my PCR test would be negative! I clung to Jesus' promise that "If you ask anything in my name, I will do it," (John 14:14) and thanked God for His Word as well as his promises. Later that morning, the phone rang. I was told to prepare to leave immediately with no further information given. My heart sank. I remembered the nurse saying that if my PCR was positive, I would leave immediately for isolation. A man ushered me out towards a waiting ambulance. "Where am I going?" I asked. "The Ritz- Carlton hotel, because your PCR is negative."

Hallelujah! I wanted to jump and shout but I got into the ambulance calmly without asking any further questions. God had delivered me from that outcome. My heart overflowed in thanksgiving for His miraculous intervention!

When I returned to the Hotel, they told me that housekeeping had packed up all my belongings and disinfected the room. They did not expect my return. Hence, to resume my quarantine, they reallocated me to a new room, a higher level with a better view.

Again, God's love! This experience has reminded me to always stand firm on God's Word and believe in His promises. To God be the glory for His gracious provision and miraculous resolution!

Praise him today. He will extend his love to you and answer your prayers.

Yen Tan

let all
you do be
done in
love

1 CORINTHIANS 16:14

Lina

BARA

Lina Bara is the wife of Domenico Bara National Overseer of the Church of God Italy. She is also a mother, an intercessor of prayer, she has been in ministry for many years and loves encouraging the younger generation to become who God has called them to be.

My name is Lina. I was born in southern Italy to parents who disagreed with each other since my birth. This affected my growth negatively from a psychological point of view.

By a miracle I met Jesus in my tender age, through my grandmother.

She was a very dear person and a sure point of reference for me and my mother, especially after she met Jesus. She was strong and courageous, a woman who had survived the war, becoming a widow at the age of forty with five children.

She would take me to church as a child in hopes it would help me know God's love. And it worked. With her certainty and hope in God, she believed that the Lord would save me from the negative future she felt for me.

I remember when I was 6-7 years old. My parents usually had a heated fight early in the morning and the punishment was that my mother would not receive any money to buy us food for that day. My sister and I had some stale bread soaked in water with a little sugar for breakfast. Mother had none.

My father didn't show up for lunch and there was only a small amount of food, stale bread for my sister. Mom and I waited until almost 16.00 (4 pm) but my father had not returned. My mom was very tired, and she didn't know what to do and I was very hungry.

She had a brilliant idea. We would walk to her sister's who lived in the neighboring town about 40-60 minutes away.

In order not to upset her, I agreed. However, my mother made a condition. We would just go for a nice visit and not for a request of food. The aunt must not suspect we were hungry but, if she offered us something to eat, we would not refuse. I accepted with the hope of food. However, it didn't go as Mom had planned. After walking far in the sun, arriving at the aunt exhausted, she only offered us fruit juice.

I was angry and hungry. All I could think about was returning home with an empty stomach. I hoped my father would bring something for supper. (He did not come home until 10pm when we were already asleep.) We didn't stay long. I wanted to go home. I walked far away from Mom and I began to cry. I was so unhappy at our life so I started talking to the Lord.

I asked Him; "Jesus, only you can do something for us. You have done it before for many people, please do it for us now too".

I reminded Him of some of his miracles as I prayed. "Please, I can't stand it anymore, I'm very hungry, persuade my father to bring us something to eat, otherwise you can do something for us." I was crying and praying and didn't realize that we were almost home. But at that very moment a boy passed by carrying bread and he dropped a loaf on the ground right by me. I picked it up and called to him that it had fallen. He said to leave it there. It could not be sold because it was now dirty. Then my spiritual eyes were opened. I heard a voice saying to me: "It's for you, take it. Take it home and eat it".

But my angry mom told me that dirty bread could not be eaten. I squeezed the bread tight and told Mom I would take it home at any cost. My mom angrily tried to make me leave it, insisting that we wouldn't eat that dirty bread. Then I begged her, saying if we made a fire and put the bread on it, all the bacteria would be gone. Then I also told her that Jesus had done this miracle for us. She was convinced, and agreed, tired of arguing. So that night we went to bed full of fresh bread.

This was the first miracle that I knew of God's love but it was the beginning of living by faith in my life. His goodness has been a shield to me in every area of my life until today at 63 years old. In the ministry, in my marriage, in our home and with all four children.

God is good! His kindness and love endures forever from age to age. Glory be to his name always!

My prayer for you:

Allow his goodness to be yours today. Amen

And
Above ALL
things
be
Earnest in your
LOVE
for among yourselves,
Love covers a
multitude of sins.

1 PETER 4:8

Vanda

CHIEGO

Vanda Chiego, widow of Pastor Giovanni LaRocchia. Today sister Vanda is leading the church in Triggiano in southern of Italy, in a secular job she is a children's teacher. Vanda has three children.

After getting married to my husband in 1992, I was expecting my first child. At 37 weeks, following a sensation of widespread itching all over my body, the doctor urgently prescribed liver tests from which a liver alteration was found. The day after the results, they urgently terminated the pregnancy and Sara was born on 2 March 1993, but I risked death due to complications in the operating room. By that time, I had already received my husband's testimony of faith, and as a Catholic catechist, after a while when I began to read the Bible. I realized that not everything was as the Catholic Church said it was, I decided not to attend any more and began my in-depth study of the scriptures.

The surgery resulted in my inability to not have any more pregnancies: the doctor made mistakes in the operating room (at the same time treating two other girls!). This affected my heart. I wanted a large family because having lost my mother at the age of 13, I wanted to compensate for that loss. But I could no longer do that.

More or less four years later, a colleague at work told me about her child she had adopted from Brazil, and I told my husband about it. The Lord had given us both dreams of children being given to us by people who had already prepared the documents! We approached an agency with which we started the adoption paperwork. God told us precisely what we had to do through people who knew nothing about the case, through prayer and the Word of God: documents to prepare, paths to take or to give up, even the country to which we should turn. And so it was. When we arrived at the orphanage in Russia in 1998, I saw the same scene I had dreamt of in a dream, confirming that we were in the place and time God had manifested. My husband and I adopted not one but two children aged 8 months and 2 years and 2 months in a supernatural way in just 6 months after the documents were sent.

The episode with the woman with the issue of the blood helped me a lot in this journey and that is to think that even though the devil was allowed to deprive me of the possibility of having other pregnancies, he did not deprive me of the possibility of becoming a mother.

Matthew 9:20, *And behold, a woman, sick of a flow of blood for twelve years, approaching him from behind, touched the hem of His garment, because she said to herself, "If I can at least touch his garment, I will be healed." Jesus turned, saw her, and said, "Take courage, child; your faith has healed you." From that hour the woman was healed.*

For 12 years she had had that hemorrhage that should have killed her in those days, but what that power did, not to have in those 12 years could not deprive her of the possibility of being healed: the Lord had other plans for her life.

And also for mine! God's love won out over so many obstacles. The family I have today, even though I no longer have my husband by my side, I know that it was planned and designed by God Himself for His plan of glory. Today Sara is 29, Alessandro 26 and Laura 23.

God bless us all!

Vanda Chiego

I AM WITH YOU

always

Matthew 28:20

Norma

RAMIREZ QUISPE

I am Norma Ramirez Quispe and 44 years old. I am from Peru but I have lived in Italy from the time I was 13 years. I have served the Lord since I was 24 years old. If I had to choose between all the miracles that God has done in my life, it would truly take a long time for there are so many.

God has been good, loving and patient in all the stages of my life from childhood to today. It is difficult to choose but I could say that God has protected me all my life. I have seen his hand be precious in each year that I have lived, although it is true that I have had some very bad days. The gray days were sometimes long but God's faithfulness was always there.

One of the greatest times of his faithfulness was when my father gave himself to the Lord. From that day, all of our family was reborn. Truly, it was a miracle my father repented because my mother was about to die.

God allowed this for a purpose. My father had a very messy life. He was constantly drunk and would hit us, especially my mother because she defended us. But the Lord gave us a great miracle by saving my father. It was one of the greatest miracles that I can see in the life of my family. As a result of that happening, our whole life was changed.

This was the favor of God. It helped me to understand more about God's ways. I then began to work for the Lord when I was 24 years old with the young people in Peru at the Assemblies of God church. I learned many things as a new daughter of the Lord under my good pastor and many friends in the church. God blessed my life to move to Italy where I would later meet my husband, Yober Regalado.

We married in 2009 and three years later we began a family. Our firstborn was Aaron. Then Abigail and later, Rebeca. We have been blessed by the Lord with all three of our children. There are no words how we feel. We follow the Lord in Italy in the Church of God and we want to do better for him as we instruct our children in the ways of the Lord.

The Lord has been faithful to us. We do not complain. He continues to be there with many miracles every day, so many it would be impossible to describe them on a page. So I say it again. Ever since I was a child, the Lord has shown his love to me.

I am confident he will continue to do so always as I obey him. Psalm 32: 3-5 is precious to me. It was my motto when I was in my 20's even when I got married, these verses still spoke to me:

"As long as I keep silent, my bones in my body moan all day. Because day and night your hand was engraved on me; my greenery became summer droughts. I declared my sin to you, and did not cover my iniquity. I said, I will confess my transgressions to Jehovah; and you forgave the wickedness of my sin."

There is another verse that also helps me. Perhaps, it will also help you.

Psalms 43:5, "Why are you cast down, oh my soul, and why are you troubled within me, wait on God because I still have to praise him, salvation is mine and my God."

Think about all he has done for you in the past. He is faithful with an extraordinary love! Let him be your friend.

Norma Ramirez Quispe

Jacqueline
MERLO

The Extraordinary Love of God manifests in his word

Jacqueline is the wife of Pastor Christian Merlo, National Overseer of the Church of God in France. She is a co-pastor, mother, grandmother and a light to many women as she leads them in victory!

The dictionary defines extraordinary as follows, remarkable, exceptional. Love is an attribute of God, love is an aspect of God's character and of his person. Love is truly the greatest force that exists and is central to the nature of God.

By his love he gives John 3:16,
"For God so loved the world, that he gave his only begotten Son, that whosoever believeth in him should not perish, but have everlasting life."

God loves us unconditionally, eternally and endlessly. God gave His only begotten Son to die for us so that we could be saved from our bondage to sin. This is true love, this is the love of God.

Like other aspects of God's character His love is limitless: it's length, it's breadth, it's height, it's depth, it's duration, it's density and it's intensity are infinite.

When the mountains recede, when the hills……..
The love of God is qualified as infallible, it is the first adjective that the Bible uses to describe the love of God.

1John 3:1-3,
"Behold what love the Father has shown us that we may be called sons of God: therefore the world does not know us, because it did not know him. Beloved, we are now sons of God, and what we will be does not yet appear; but we know that when he appears we will be like him; for we shall see him as he is. And everyone who has this hope in him purifies himself, as he is pure."

Love is truly the greatest force that exists and is central to the nature of God. He is greater than the cruellest evil and he triumphs over sin and death.
The death of our Lord and Savior Jesus Christ on the cross, in order to become sin in our place, is a visible example of the invisible (but ever more real) love of God.

Romans 5:6-8,

> *"For when we were yet without strength, Christ, in due time,*
> *died for the ungodly. Hardly would one die for a just man; maybe*
> *someone would die for a good man. But God proves his love*
> *toward us, in that, while we were still sinners, Christ died for us."*

His love has been so real to me the many years of my life until this present day. He has kept my loved ones, healed my children many times and continues to show his love to my family today. Truly, there is no explanation for Christ's love except, extraordinary!

Jacqueline Merlo

Love is Patient, Love is Kind.

It does not envy, it does not boast, it is not proud.
It does not dishonor others, it is not self-seeking,
it is not easily angered, it keeps no record of wrongs.
Love does not delight in evil but rejoices with the *truth.*
It always *protects,* always *trusts,*
always *hopes,* always *perseveres.*

Love never fails.

And now these three remain:
faith, hope, and *love.*
But the greatest of these is love.

I CORINTHIANS 13:4-8,13

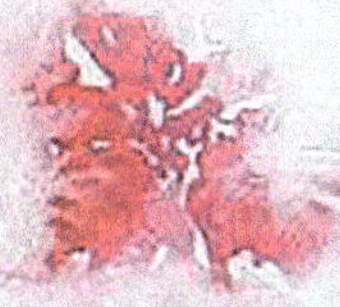

Christiane

KENNEL

Christiane Kennel is the wife of Pastor Francis Kennel, Bar-sur-Aube, France She is the mother of three children and has two grandchildren of German origin. She lives in France and works with disabled children at school.

I was recently touched by the love of God our father for us, his children! Indeed, we have seen that God answers the prayers of previous generations and we have seen the fulfillment of the following verse in Isaiah 55:11; *"So is my word that goes out from my mouth: It will not return to me empty, but will accomplish what I desire and achieve the purpose for which I sent it."*

With my husband, we have been pastors for 18 years of a small church in France. We are in the Champagne region in the middle of the countryside, where the Catholic religion is very present and rooted in the life of the villagers.

We have welcomed and accompany a large number of people of different nationalities as well as many refugees. But for many reasons, these people were forced to leave our region to settle in the big cities. This church has been marked by the "departures and arrivals" of people since its foundation.

More than once we found ourselves restarting the work at church with only a handful of people and often a feeling of discouragement seized us. But our Lord taught us that He expected us to be faithful in the task He entrusted to us, even if with our human eyes we did not see the result. Precisely, we were contacted recently several times to do funerals for people who were looking for a Protestant pastor.

The story began 80 years ago, when my husband's grandfather, also a pastor, crisscrossed the area on Sundays on horseback, going from farm to farm to celebrate the Sunday service. Christians having no fixed place of worship at the time, gathered every Sunday in different farms. From this period there remained the childhood memory of the word of God in these elderly people close to death today.

God watched over His Word, the prayers of parents and grandparents at that time and allowed us to benefit today from God's love and faithfulness to his children. We were able to take to repentance some of these elderly people who have throughout their lives neglected their relationship with God and we see also their children to be challenged by this faith and come to church now.

For me it was such a proof of God's love for his children. Indeed, his word does not return to him without having carried out his will. Thus we also see the answering of the prayers of previous generations, often already deceased. I am touched by this love of our Father who does not want any sinners to perish, but for all to come to eternal life. In the parable of the prodigal son (Luke 15,11-32), we see that the father waits every day for the return of his son. Also in the parable of the lost sheep (Luke 15,1-7), where the good shepherd leaves the 99 sheep to look for the only lost sheep until he finds it!

The love of God is such that He cares for each of us, even the one who dwells deep in the countryside to bring Him back to Him. This last experience showed me how nothing is lost for God: - Neither the prayers made for one of our children, family or a friend and which do not yet seem to be answered, nor the word of God preached and announced for years!!!

I encourage you to proclaim His word about your family, children, friends or ministry, for He will accomplish what He has promised!
Do not forget this truth:

"Train a child in the way he should go, and when he is old,
he will not turn from it."
Proverbs 22:6

"So is my word that goes out from my mouth: It will not return
to me empty, but will accomplish what I desire and achieve the
purpose for which I sent it."
Isaiah 55:11

Christiane Kennel

faith
CAN MOVE
mountains.

Annette

HORNING

Finding the Father's love

Annette Horning, born in South Africa, is the wife of Steve Horning, missionary for 45 years and mother of three children; ages, 28, 42 and 43. They have lived in South America, North America and Thailand. She and Steve have planted churches on three continents but have lived in Andorra for the past 23 years as pastors. Annette met her husband in Montreal in 1976.

I grew up with a father who didn't know how to love me. He was a father who had many of his own personal problems and my very loving mother suffered a lot because of my father. Since I didn't have a loving earthly father I needed a father's love. When I accepted Jesus into my life, I had to learn about the love of my heavenly father.

The first thing I learned was that I couldn't earn my heavenly father's love by what I did or didn't do. God's love is unconditional. I realized his desire for me was first to understand him above all, and then to understand the difference between a father and a loving father.

Two and a half years after I came to know the Lord I asked him to show me my own heart. Why? I knew that the heart is deceitful above all things. So I asked.

He did reveal to me what my heart was like and I became so sad that I cried a whole day just seeing my heart's condition. I felt broken! But, being broken at that moment helped me to understand and accept God's love in my heart even more.

For the first time I was able to love myself and love others with the love of God. I now understood his love for me was genuine and real. I could reach out to others with His love and not my own. This is what the Lord desires for us to understand and experience for ourselves. When we accept the extraordinary love of Jesus, we can then love one another.

Through brokenness my life was changed! I learned that I needed to do things through my heavenly father's strength, not my own strength in trying to please him.

Jeremiah 9:24 says,

> *"But let him who glories glory in this,*
> *that he understands and knows me,*
> *that I am the Lord exercising loving-kindness,*
> *judgement, and righteousness in the earth.*
> *For in these I delight, says the Lord."*

My prayer for you:

That all of us will find that his love
is enough in each of our lives.

His grace is sufficient
2 CORINTHIANS 12:9

Annette Horning

Ghertie

NOE

True Love: God

Ghertie is the wife of Renzo Noe', National Overseer of the Church of God in Sweden. She is a mother and pastora alongside her husband of the Spanish speaking church in Stockholm. Although she holds a full time job, she loves serving the Lord, to worship and strengthen others to become God's best.

I want to write about the true and extraordinary love of God.

But because the love of God surpasses all understanding, I feel absolutely inadequate. I do know with the guidance of the Holy Spirit we can glimpse the unfathomable love of God.

The very essence of God is love. God is much greater, more sublime than we can imagine, and so is his love. Many times our human love is petty, limited and selfish. God's love is immense, it has no limits and it is extraordinary! My experience with the love of God is daily. Regardless of my mood or the moment I am living, I can experience the love of God.

Psalm 143:11-12,
"For your name Lord, give me life; for your justice get me out of this predicament. For your great love, destroy my enemies; kill my opponents."

This means that His love, justice and grace do not depend on what I have done or said. It doesn't depend on anything I do; whether I go to all the church meetings, whether I sang well or not, or whether I do charity work or even pray many hours a day.

For me, the greatest act of love that exists is the cross and I could write thousands of columns talking about this topic. This would be for me and many believers the most important thing of our faith.

The cross of Jesus Christ is central to the Christian faith. The cross reveals to us the character of God: his love for lost sinners and his perfect justice meet at the cross.

If we want to grow in our love for God, which is the first and greatest commandment, then we must be growing in understanding and appreciating the cross. This shows us his great love. Nothing is impossible with Jesus and all sin is cleansed at the cross. The cross means life. The man who is dead rises to eternal life.

We receive his love by faith and not by works. Jesus' sacrifice has already been given on the cross. He became the first fruits of eternal life. He made it possible to have direct access to communion with God, the Father. There are no intermediaries necessary; such as priests, virgins or saints who intercede for us. Just Jesus!

More helpful scriptures for you to read:
Deliverance from guilt and sin (Romans 3:19)
Free from the chains of the devil
Heals from sickness and suffering (Psalms 31)
Heals anxiety and fear (John 4: 18)
Overcome death (Romans 6:23; and Revelations 21:8)

What a contrast between the love of Jesus and the curse of the thorns! Thanks to the fact that he carried our curse, we can overcome anxiety and fear. We can have the conviction that He loves us and will love us until it is the last day of our lives. His extraordinary love waits for you!

Cherlie Noe

Valerie

MORALES

Valerie grew up in Uruguay, in 2013 she moved to Sweden and helped to connect the church with the Church of God.

From a very young age I knew the love of God. When I was a few months old, my older sister and I were diagnosed with an incurable disease, with no chance of survival. It was there that God showed his immense love to our family and performed a miracle by completely healing us.

Although I was always aware of this, I never really understood what God's love was until I arrived in Sweden. I arrived in 2013 with a lot of dreams and goals. I was just married, leaving everything behind to start a new life with my husband. At first everything was new and fascinating. As the days began to pass, as my husband worked all day, loneliness and the feeling that something was missing began to grow in my life. As the days passed, it felt like there was no one to call or to go have a coffee with. There wasn't even anybody to go for a walk with. I felt that nothing could fill that feeling of sadness caused by being away from my loved ones. I began to study and occupy my mind with different things. Nothing filled that void.

Until one day, alone in my apartment, God embraced me with His immense love. A unique experience. He made me feel that I needed nothing more than Him, than his love. That feeling was so great and so immense that I knew I only needed God to be complete. It was him and me, and I didn't need anything else. That day marked a "before and after." From that day on it is his love that sustains me in every situation. It is His love that lifts me up in my difficult moments and that completes me every day. No matter what trials come, his love is enough to get me through anything.

God loves me so much that He has given me a beautiful family, a home full of peace, a church that is like my family, and has surrounded me with people who bless me in every way. Today I can only thank God, because His will has brought me here, and it is His love what has sustained me along the way. I know that this same love will continue to support me, and it will also support my daughters and my husband daily.

That encounter with Him changed the way I see and feel about His love for me. Today His love is not only something I have heard about but it became reality instead and the pillar of my life!

May we never lack the love of God!

Valerie Morale

Lidia

ROSADO

Agape love = Unconditional love

Lidia Rosado is the wife of Jaime Rosado, the National Overseer of the Church of God in Portugal. She serves as co-pastor beside her husband. She is a mother and grandmother and is loved by all the women as she leads them in God's unconditional love.

I thought I would tell you a little bit about Agape LOVE being a specific type of love. Agape love is very important in the Bible. In the New

Testament alone it appears 158 times. Agape love is not just about feeling or doing this or that, it is an act of obedience, with the purpose of doing good to those who in this world do not know it exists. A love that works and that can be evidenced by the relationship that Jesus has with the Father and with us (John 3:16; John 13:34-35).

We can say that the origin of this love is in the Lord himself. An unconditional, perfect, sacrificial love! As we are imperfect beings, this kind of love cannot originate in us. But it can be generated in us by the Holy Spirit. Only in this way can we love as the Lord loves (Romans 5:5; 1 John 3:16; Galatians 5:22).

On the cross of Calvary we can see God's unconditional love for us, where we can see God's agape love for us with Jesus' sacrifice, because agape love is always visible (John 3:16-18).

We are not worthy of such love from the Lord: "
But God demonstrates his love for us: while we were yet sinners,
Christ died for us."
Romans 5:8

Agape love is no respecter of people, it made me a different person, wherever I walk, I have to show God's great love in my life. And when I let the agape love flood my heart there is a great "attunement" and intimacy with God.

I was born in a Christian home but that doesn't give me the label of being the King's daughter. I had to admit that I was a sinner. The word of God is very clear that tells us that it is only possible to reach God through Jesus Christ who is alive, and who is always by our side ready to hear us, forgive and set us free as well as to heal and strengthen us!!!

That's what happened in my life! I then understood that only through Jesus I could reach the presence of God. The most important thing in all of our lives is to have a more direct and intimate coexistence with the "Lord Jesus." I want to always have intimacy with God through this extraordinary LOVE.

This is called "Tune and Intimacy" and I feel blessed for that. When I put God above anything in my life...I experience a life full of UNCONDITIONAL LOVE!!!

Jesus himself tells us that we must love God in all spheres of our existence, with all our heart, with all our soul, with all our understanding and with all our strength. Love with everything we are and have!

LOVE is a Flower...
The Flower symbolizes beauty, perfection, glory and the joy of life...
A smile, a hug, a prayer, a gesture of affection...
But also a surrender to God,

My prayer for you:

YOU BE THE FIRST FLOWER of Love!

Em nome de Jesus. Amém!

Lidia Rosado

·DRAW NEAR·
to God
AND HE WILL DRAW
NEAR TO YOU
James 4.8

Mel

BESERRA

Mel Beserra, 38 years old, Brazilian, servant, wife, daughter and pastor at the Church of God Porto/, Portugal together with my husband André Evangelista.

I felt very honored to know that I could contribute to this beautiful project. My heart was filled with joy when I was given the task of speaking about the extraordinary Love of God. In the course of the Christian walk, we hear many testimonies of how the Lord has transformed lives, healed people, and reached with his infinite mercy. When we hear the testimonies, we rejoice and our hearts are warmed with such gratitude to God for all he has done, but nothing like having your own experiences, nothing like having personally experienced this extraordinary love.

During these 23 years of conversion, I was able to experience this love. To see all His promises being fulfilled one by one to me. I came from a very humble background, I was a teenager with no perspective on life, full of trauma. I grew up in a wooden shack in what we call a favela in Brazil, my brothers, my mother and my father. Panic lived in our house, my father was an alcoholic and very violent. My mother carried the marks of this violence in her body and in her mind, My father used to drink almost every day and looked for excuses to hurt us.

A teenager molded to live a life of darkness, but in the midst of chaos the Lord reached out to me, brought me light and a life full of peace and hope. Even in difficult times I knew and felt the hand of the Lord was working in my favor, He changed my story. If I have the opportunity to write these words today it's because He made an incredible transformation in me and continues to do so. An extraordinary love that not only heals the body, but also the soul. A love that restores our emotions and restores the way we see all things.

Exactly today, the Lord spoke to me again in John 5, this passage describes a man that for 38 years was paralyzed, this passage tells us that, like many other sick people, that man was in the pool of Bethesda (House of Mercy), waiting for the waters to be stirred up by an angel and the first one who managed to enter would receive the cure.

Jesus was totally unknown to this man, however, this paralyzed man was not unknown to Jesus. Jesus saw this man, and not only saw him, but also knew all the time of his suffering, and asks him a question that could change his state. The paralyzed man thought that his cure would come by the means he believed were the most viable. Perhaps he said: "I can only be healed by the normal means I'm used to. My healing will only come my way, the way I believe, by my paradigms."

Perhaps he said more: "I know there is a possibility, but nobody helps me and nobody understands me!"

Jesus called this man to be healed of his paralysis that only made him see that reality. The paralysis kept him lying down, which only made him see that tank. The paralysis did not allow him to see new horizons. Indeed, for those who had not yet had an experience with Jesus, the hope of healing lies in getting into that pool. However, for the paralytic who was seen by Jesus, his healing now depended on him listening and obeying what Jesus said to him: "Get up, take up your bed and walk!"

This was unlike anything he'd ever tried. It went against all his beliefs and concepts. Against everything he's ever seen and experienced. That paralytic, like me and thousands, thousands of people, experienced such great love, this extraordinary love that constrains us every day.

Mel Beserra

GOD SURROUNDS ME WITH HIS favor
PSALM 5:12

Shakila

OLSEN

Saved by His love!

Shakila Olsen is the wife of John Olsen, the National Overseer of the Church of God in Netherlands. She is a mother of three, an anointed speaker and serves as co- pastor alongside her husband at "Send the Light" Amsterdam. Shakila loves to serve the Lord and ALL the people around her.

I grew up in a family that suffered domestic violence. My father drank a lot, and when he came home, he would hit my mother, but he never hit us children when he was drunk. I grew up in this environment, not knowing any better.

We practiced the Hindu religion in our home. On the days when my father came home drunk and hit my mother, I would hide in my wardrobe. I would put my hands over my ears and pray to the Hindu gods to stop the violence. But nothing happened!

I finally stood up against my father at age 19. I told him to stop beating my mother, and he did at that moment. He never expected me to go against him. However, after that day, he began to abuse me emotionally with bad words that penetrated deep into my heart.

A thought was then planted in my head and I now know it was by satan. I decided I did not want to live anymore and didn't want to go on like this. Maybe my father would change when I was gone.

So one evening, I took a lot of pills hoping not to wake up the next day. This thought became my deepest desire. Fortunately for me, there was someone who thought differently.

I woke up in the middle of the night and was violently ill. When I went back to bed, I started to cry. I cried out from the deepest parts of my heart to all the gods that came to my mind; allah, krishna, buddha, etc., and even to Jesus.

Jesus heard my cry. He was there listening to me that night. Psalms 33: 13-15 says, *"...God looks from heaven to all the children of men...."*

Shortly after my suicide attempt, I met my husband, John. I left home and we moved in together quite quickly (we were not Christians at that time). But God had a plan. John soon became acquainted with Jesus Christ and gave his heart to the Lord. Shortly afterward, the Lord also allowed me to experience His love, peace, and freedom. His extraordinary love went through my whole body. I felt it in every cell throughout all of my being. The only thing I could say was, "Yes, Jesus, I want you." I had never experienced such love before. At the same time that I felt his love and immediately began to sing and speak in new tongues. I was instantly baptized in the Holy Spirit.

Wow, amazing love! A love that cannot be found on this earth. God made me feel whole, that I was worthy, that I was wanted, and that He loved me.

Nothing is too great for our Lord. By His love, I was saved. By His love, you, too, can be saved. He can do everything for you. We only have to say, "Yes, Lord," and He will do it.

My prayer for you:

That you stay blessed and be blessed in God's extraordinary love!

Shakila Olsen

BE
STRONG
IN
THE
LORD
Ephesians 6:10

Nanny

BENJAMINS-TOMBENG

Where love dwells, the Lord commands His blessing - Psalm 133:3

Nanny Benjamins recently retired from her pastorship. She is now an advisor to the new leadership team and is still active within the Church of God, The Netherlands council. She is married to Mike and has one son and grandmother of three grandchildren.

How wonderful it is to know that you are loved. When I look back at my childhood in Indonesia, I am assured that God's love was already at work in my young life. I come from a family of eight children, six girls and two boys, of whom I am number four. My father was a full-time minister for the Lord. My mother was a praying woman. What I learned from my parents is that God is always there.

My first memory as a little girl of 3 or 4 years old, I had an accident. A solid wooden bench fell on my foot and I was hospitalised. My parents visited me every day. Whenever they were about to go home, tears started to flow. A child instinctively feels that he/she is safe and loved by his/her parents. I only wanted to be with them because that made me feel calm. Just like a plant needs water and sunlight, I felt I only needed the love of my parents.

When I was 13 years old, I had given my life to Christ. At the end of a divine service an altar call was made and I went to the front of the altar. There I experienced for the first time the immeasurable love of God for me. I felt washed clean, cleansed from head to toe. This encounter with Christ is indescribably intense and beautiful. I could only weep for joy and thank Him for His forgiveness - I felt new and reborn. It is like the Bible passage in John 3 verse 3 where Christ told Nicodemus that unless one is born again, he cannot see the Kingdom of God.

The love of God worked in my teenage years in such a way that I realized that wherever I am, His eyes are on me. What a comfort that God is with me in His love.

As I left the room where my husband and I had held our wedding party, my mother's eyes caught mine. Only then did it dawn on me that I was entering a new phase of life. I closed the door of my parental home behind me. Childhood, the years of adolescence flew by. A new chapter of my life opened. ABBA Father blessed us soon with a son whom we were allowed to lovingly raise in the fear of the Lord.

When God called me to be a pastor in our church, I had quit my job at a large telecom company. The love of God was my guide, my inspiration not only to come to this decision, but also to remain faithful in the many ups and downs of congregational life.

It is an honor to work for God, to pass on God's love in word and deed. To pray for the needs; to see healings take place in Jesus name, also in my personal life where God healed me from cancer; to see how God provides both in material and spiritual matters.

Knowing that I am loved by the Lord is my anchor. The best thing that has happened to me - the love of God!

My prayer for you:

I pray and proclaim that the same may happen to you. Let the words of Psalm 133 verse 3 be your motto: *"Where love dwells, the LORD commands His blessing."*

Nanny Benjamins-Toteng

WATCH!
STAND FIRM IN THE FAITH!
BE COURAGEOUS!
BE STRONG!
1 CORINTHIANS 16:13

Jacqueline

ROUVOET

My name is Jacqueline Rouvoet and together with my husband Frits, I lead the work of Bright Fame where we reach women and men who are working behind the window (prostitutes) in the Red Light District of Amsterdam and whom we want to help to get out of prostitution and build a new life.

I believed in God from a young age and when I first heard about missionaries, I knew I wanted to be a missionary. I was very surprised when, at the age of 10, I was swinging on the swing with a boyfriend, that he said he didn't want to marry me because I wanted to become a missionary. I thought that everyone wanted to be a missionary.

IF ANY OF YOU LACK

WISDOM,

LET HIM ASK OF GOD,

THAT GIVETH TO ALL MEN LIBERALLY,

AND UPBRAIDETH NOT; AND IT SHALL BE GIVEN HIM.

BUT LET HIM ASK IN

FAITH,

NOTHING WAVERING.

FOR HE THAT WAVERETH IS LIKE A

WAVE OF THE SEA

DRIVEN WITH THE WIND AND TOSSED.

JAMES 1:5-6

Mary
CARMEN

Hello dear sisters,

Mary Carmen Gomez is the wife of Jaume Torrado, National Overseer of the Church of God of Spain. She loves Jesus, is a mother and grandmother. Her life ambition is to serve the Lord and encourage the body of Christ, especially the women, through God's love.

It is a privilege to be able to share about the love of God! God is Love! This is one of the most beautiful, wonderful and profound truths of the Bible.

1 John: 4:9-10 declares:

*"…God is love. In this the love of God was shown toward us, that
God sent his only begotten Son into the world, that we might live
through him. In this is love: not that we loved God, but that he
loved us and sent his Son to be the propitiation for our sins."*

Since I received Jesus in my heart at the age of 19, I have always felt
and seen the Love of God in my life and also, in the life of my family.

At all times and in all circumstances! Even now in these moments of
my life as I am going through health problems, I have never stopped seeing
his wonderful Love.

In Ephesians 3:18-19, I found the most beautiful verse in the bible
about the Love of God:

*"Be fully capable of understanding with all the saints what is
width, length, depth, and height, and to know the love of Christ,
which surpasses all knowledge, so that you may be filled with all
the fullness of God."*

God is love in all its dimensions, His love is so perfect that it is
difficult to define it with our words, it has no limit, it is infinite, He loved
us with an eternal love.

He loves you dear sister. He is right there beside you. His love will
carry you through each and every situation in your life.

My prayer for you:

Ask him right now to bring you peace and his love. He is near to you!

Mary Carmen Gómez

Ana

DOMINGUEZ

Ana Dominguez pastors together with her husband at the Iglesia de Dios Vida Cristiana in Valencia, Spain. She loves the Lord and proclaims His Love to all.

I will never forget March 14, 2020, the day we were asked to go into confinement in Spain. Overnight, we were locked in our home without really knowing what we were hiding from, where the virus was and how we could fight it.

It has been more than a year since that happened and we are still living the restrictions that the pandemic has brought us. For many it has meant fear, for others, insecurity, and for others, mourning.

For me it has been a mixture of feelings, some positive and many negative. However, Romans 8:28, "And we know that God makes all things work together for the good of those who love him and are called according to his purpose for them," has been an answer to my lowest moments.

In this verse, God reminds me that he is sovereign to give me comfort and strength in the midst of all trials. He rules and I can rest in his good, pleasing, and perfect will, and those of us who love God can be sure that God is carrying out his purpose in us.

Difficult times are times of new opportunities, of new challenges. These are times when God shapes the character of Christ in us. And we can say like the apostle Paul: *"Brothers, I myself do not pretend to have already achieved it; but one thing I do: Forgetting what is left behind and reaching out to what is ahead, I press on to the goal, to the prize of the high calling of God in Christ Jesus."* Philippians 3:13-14.

I believe that if we change our focus, if we learn to live "extending ourselves to what is ahead", we will be preparing the ground for better days, we will be stronger, our vision will be sharper, and our horizon will expand. We will recognize the opportunities. Our spiritual senses will be more sensitive.

In the midst of every difficult situation, God is going to provide us with unique opportunities, but if our eyes are not looking ahead, we will not recognize them, they will pass us by and we will not take advantage of them. In the Bible, there are many examples of men and women who in the midst of their difficulty seized opportunities: Ruth, being a widow and a foreigner, knew how to take advantage of the opportunity to work in Boaz's field.

Joseph, while in prison, took the opportunity to interpret a dream. David, in the middle of the war, seized the opportunity to kill the giant. They all focused on what was in front of them and that opportunity changed their lives forever.

I have discovered two enemies of vision: The first is complaint. Complaining keeps us walking in circles around our difficulty, does not allow us to take our eyes off the problem and prevents us from recognizing opportunities.

Another enemy is memories, good and bad. The bad memories discourage us and undermine our faith; the good ones entertain and distract us. Let us learn to "certainly forget what is left behind", the past should only remind us how far God has brought us and how he has sustained us, but let us not allow the past to prevent us from seeing the horizon that God is drawing before us.

Everything we are experiencing will pass and better times will come, but those who have seized the opportunities will be enjoying the fruit of their vision.

My prayer for you:

Let God's love continue to hold you in your everyday life.

Ana Domínguez

I CAN DO
ALL THINGS
THROUGH
Christ
WHO GIVES ME
STRENGTH
- PHILIPPIANS 4:13 -

Juani

ALVAREZ

Hello everyone. My name is Juani. I am 54 years old and I want to talk to you about the love and goodness of God in my life as well as in the life of my family.

I experienced the love of God in my teens at the age of 13 when I understood how much God loved me by giving his only son, Jesus Christ to die on a cross to forgive my sins and give me salvation with eternal life.

From the age of 13 until today, when I am 54, in my life experience with the Lord I can only say that his love and kindness have always accompanied us, both me and my family. God has shown us His great love and faithfulness at all times.

I want to share with you some things that God has done in our lives. One of the ways that God showed us His love and power is that when I was converted, God did a miracle with my health. I was physically limited. I had chronic asthmatic bronchitis. I couldn't run like other children, I suffocated. When this happened, I thought I was going to die. My parents spent a lot of money on specialist doctors to improve my health, but without any success. I was still having many crises, until Jesus healed me of this disease.

Another way God showed His goodness to me is that He answered my fervent prayer that my parents and two sisters would know the Lord. At the age of 25, God gave me a wonderful husband and today we have three beautiful children who also gave their lives to Christ, the fruit of another answered prayer.

We have constantly been able to see and experience the love of God in our lives. I could recount many experiences of all these years that we have walked with him but it would be untrue if I said that everything was easy. We have been through trials, difficulties, sorrows, pain, joys, economic and family losses. Through it all, we can say with total conviction that God has been with us. His love and fidelity have never left us.

Romans 8: 35-39:
> *"Who shall separate us from the love of Christ? Tribulation or*
> *anguish or persecution or famine or nakedness or peril or sword?*
> *As it is written, because of you we are killed all the time, we are*
> *counted as sheep to the slaughter, but in all these things we are*
> *more than conquerors through him who loved us, for which,*
> *I am sure that not even death, neither life, nor angels, nor*
> *principalities, nor powers, neither things present nor things to*
> *come, neither height nor depth, nor any other created thing, will*
> *be able to separate us from the love of God which is in Christ Jesus*
> *our Lord."*

Nothing and no one can separate us from his love because he loves us with an eternal love. His great love has so captivated our hearts that we only want to be with him and live for him.

I hope that by sharing my experience with God I can bless and encourage you today to always trust His love.

My prayer for you:

God will be there for you, just ask Him!

A hug from Spain / Un abrazo desde España,

IT IS GOD
WHO ARMS
ME WITH
STRENGTH
AND KEEPS
MY WAY
SECURE.
2 Samuel 22:33

Denise

LIZ TSHITEYA

I am First Lady Denise "Liz" Tshiteya, wife of thirty years of Bishop Jean T. Tshiteya, pastor and founder of the "La Nouvelle Jerusalem" church in Liège. Pastor Jean is the National Overseer of the Church of God in Belgium; he is also Director of Youth and Christian Education for the Church of God in Western Europe. I am a mother of four children (two young boys and two young girls) and a journalist by training.

How can we not testify of what God does and His faithfulness? How can we not push people to attach themselves to Him and serve Him?

We don't do it enough because we often don't understand His ways, His way of talking to us and protecting us. So, we often think that He has abandoned us, that He does not answer us, that He does not work on us when He actually does it.

We were two sisters, inseparable as the fingers of the hand, unable to argue and who were sharing everything, even the most intimate things. The only time we have had some communication difficulties has been when I accepted the Lord; she was very cartesian and knew nothing about the Christian life.

My sister, two and a half years older than me, nevertheless ended up joining me in the great family of Christ. I had the privilege of seeing my future husband lead her to the Lord Jesus and continue to mentor her over the years. Very quickly, she found herself deeply committed to her church, serving the Lord with incredible zeal and consecration, as if she did not have a moment to waste, as if her time was running out.

One morning, while a wedding was being prepared in her church, she decided to go buy a certain fish that the bride-to-be loved very much. She dropped off her two-year-old daughter with her pastor's wife and went shopping. On the way back, more or less 5 kilometers from where she was going to take back her daughter, she had a violent car accident: a frontal impact that was fatal to her. Her car caught fire, no one managed to save her, and that day she left to join her Lord.

What a pain when, at home, I received a phone call from my friend (her pastor's wife) who asked me," "Do you know?" I replied, "Of what?" A long silence after which she just uttered a name "... Maleta".

Everything revolved around me, it was as if my chest was torn off in an instant, I saw my future collapse in front of me because even our studies we had done them in relation to each other in order to complement each other in our business. Alone at home, I was waiting to get out of this bad dream, but I didn't wake up. So I was going to have to live without her? Yes: she had burned in her car and my father who was an orthopedic surgeon, was not allowed to see what was left of her. Someone must be wondering how this testimony can be encouraging. It is because despite the situation, God winked to show that He was indeed in control. The only thing that came out virtually intact from that charred car was my sister's Bible. And in this Bible there were many small papers written in her own handwriting.

The following verses:
Philippians 4:6-7, *"Worry not about anything; but in all things make your needs known to God through prayers and supplications, with thanksgiving. And the peace of God, which surpasses all understanding, will keep your hearts and thoughts in Jesus Christ."*

When I opened that Bible, it was as if God Himself was telling me not to worry, despite what I was going through. Also, the peace that inhabited me in all this trial was incredibly supernatural; no doubt that it was poured into me by God Himself. There I understood so clearly why my sister had served her God with such enthusiasm: she must have felt without realizing it that she had little time to do it! When she left, I had no regrets that "I should have told her this or that." We had told each other everything without hiding anything. We said to each other and showed ourselves how much we loved each other.

And last but not least, I had been able to bring her to the Lord, lead her on the path of salvation and I was at peace, knowing that she was now happy with her God whom she loved so much! Let us love each other and live a good life! No, God does not always act as we think, or when or by whom, or in the way one wants Him to act. But one thing is certain and that is,

My prayer for you:

He loves you so much that He will do all things for your good. He will sustains you, let Him do it!

Denise Liz Tshiteya

Your
grace
is
sufficient

2 Corinthians 12:9

Ornella

KAZUNGU

My name is Ornella. Twenty-nine years ago I was born in Burundi but I now live in the Grand Duchy of Luxembourg since January 18, 2010. I am married, a mother of a little girl and work full time in administration. My life in Jesus began 12 years ago. Today, I am a member of El Shaddai Church where I serve in worship and in Sunday school.

I am the result of the chance of an out-of-wedlock relationship between a Muslim mother and a pseudo-Catholic father, who didn't intend to be my parents. Eldest daughter of my father and second on my mother's side (she already had a son), I was raised by my paternal grandparents as if I was their own child. I was loved and pampered but received a strict and severe education in which mistakes were not allowed.

When I was 9 years old, my aunt, who was taking care of me, went to Europe. It was a big turning point in my life. Indeed, she was taking on a lot of responsibilities for me: education, food, clothes, birthday presents, … But despite the distance, she still continued to support me and kept on hearing from me. Her absence was far too heavy to bear, especially in the midst of adolescence. Deep down inside, I resented her because she was dear to me. She was my landmark and now she was gone.

As a form of blackmail concerning my aunt's help, I was falsely accused of having defamed my grandparents, of disclosing the secrets of the house and of not having made my confirmation after my catholic baptism and communion.

After these events, it was the descent into hell. The one person who I had to consider as a father, found himself without a job and without unemployment benefits. When he came to visit us regularly, I would cry when he left. I was an extra shame on the list of the mistakes in his journey and he regretted my very existence.

I felt a deep emptiness, a mere shadow of myself. It was then I started to ask myself, "What is life for? ….why all this unhappiness? …why do I even exist? ". I began to feel deep down that I was not a child like the others. I was looking for the unknown. In other words: I was wondering about my identity. Who I really was.

Without landmarks, I began to want to be like others and I envied all my friends who lived with their parents. Unconsciously, I wanted to do everything to resemble them. This wasn't possible, since we were not living in the same reality. It was legitimate for them to have breakfast and dinner at the table with their parents. I didn't feel I deserved it, but I felt I had to earn it to be able to have it.

Life was full of demands and tension, which required rigor in each of my actions. I needed help more than ever. I tried to take refuge in nightclubs and alcohol, but of course I couldn't.

God saw me. He allowed me to come to Europe at the age of 16. All I needed then was to have a new life, to start a new chapter. Somehow I knew the Lord had heard me and was reaching out to me. His love would soon be shown strong in my life.

I discovered El Shaddai Church through a mother who has since became like my own. Pastor Adama (peace be upon him) welcomed me as a father. He became a father to me for the first time. I was able to have a family and the parents that I had been waiting for so long. The Lord met me with His love on my road to Damascus.

To all who are reading this testimony of God's love, remember this one thing: If He did it for me, He can and will do it for you too.

Joel 2:25-27, *"I will restore to you the years that the swarming locust has eaten, the hopper, the destroyer, and the cutter, my great army, which I sent among you. You shall eat in plenty and be satisfied, and praise the name of the LORD your God, who has dealt wondrously with you. And my people shall never again be put to shame. You shall know that I am in the midst of Israel, and that I am the LORD your God and there is none other."*

Ornella Kazungu

His
love
gives
life

JOHN 10:10-11

Kathy
WATSON SWIFT

Restoring Love

Kathy Watson Swift is an author, motivational speaker, minister, missionary and founder/CEO of a 26 year non-profit organization that currently has an active 16 year old humanitarian project in Kenya, Africa. She is a mother and grandmother to her family as well as to many others. She serves alongside her husband, Bishop Chris Swift, the Superintendent of The Church of God (Cleveland Tennessee) in Western Europe. Kathy serves as the Women's Director for all the ladies of 13 countries and three islands.

I had given up! Once, I had known love, but no longer. That precious gift of companionship, of love for another. That love had vanished twenty two years ago when my husband had died with terminal cancer and I had been left at age 39 with one nine year old and two teenagers.

Oh yes, I had searched and even thought to myself, "Surely someday I will love again." I was still young, but to no avail no one came into my life. Now, after many years, my only focus was to do the will of God, share his love with others and to be content.

It was September and I had to attend a meeting for all missionaries in the states. I really did not want to attend but being loyal to my commitment, I did. I slipped in, sat by myself and began to listen.

Very soon a tall man came to the podium to share a topic on the program. My mind wandered, I really wanted to leave but at that very moment I heard someone whisper, "He's going to ask you out."

I jumped in my seat. "No way," I said aloud. I looked all around but there was no one sitting close by. I then looked up to the sky and said, "No way God. I am not interested."

But alas, standing with a group of friends the next evening, I found him not only standing by my side but asking me out to get a cup of coffee. Because I had heard the whisper of the Lord in my ear earlier and discovered he was a single missionary as well, I said yes. Why? I had learned he was from Europe and I lived in Africa. Logically, I knew the two could not come together, so I was safe. It would be fine.

That was before the coffee date. As I sat across from him at the table trying to listen, I found myself lost in his eyes. Never had I seen such depth as in those blue eyes, full of love and kindness, understanding and compassion. I knew right then that I was in trouble!

The next several months brought many hours of prayer for both of us as well as long distance conversations but.... one year later, we were married. Chris had lost his wife 12 years earlier in death so just like me, he had been alone long enough to know what losing love meant. Both of us had lost but had not stopped serving or working for the Lord. We had made a difficult decision to be happy for others, but perhaps, be single forever.

Romans 8:28 says, *"And we know that in all things God works for the good of those who love Him, who have been called according to his purpose."*

Yes, we both were called. Yes, we both had lost but our heart for God's work had not stopped. Yet, part of us deep within was empty from the companionship that we daily missed. But GOD!

He saw us, he knew our hearts and then "Love" found us. His restoring love came into our lives. That love would also touch countless thousands that we would minister to together as well as bring great love to both of our families.

His infinite love still continues in our lives today, ten years later. My dear sisters, do not ever give up. Hold fast, continue on. His love will hold you, surround you and keep you. Be ready for his love to restore your life in whatever area that you lack.

Prayer:

Thank you Lord that your agape love never fails. You know us and see us as we are. Oh, how we love you and wish for all to know that precious love of yours as their own.

Amen.

Kathy Watson Swift

freedomhmin.org

I have loved you with an everlasting love

Who do you say Jesus is?

We have read together these few devotions. We have seen how each person has believed or received God's extraordinary love. Now, we ask a question of you, what do you believe about God's love?

Do you know this Jesus we have talked about?

Many people believe He is real but have never experienced his love for themselves. In the Bible Jesus asked Peter, who was His disciple, this question;

"Who do you say I am?"

Peter replied;

"Thou are the Christ, the son of the living God."
Matthew 16:16

We believe that Jesus is the giver of life, our redeemer.

His love is FREE!

It is our prayer that if you do not know him, today will be your day to ask forgiveness. Right now you can accept His love and friendship allowing Him to be Lord of your life.

Pray with me these words:

Dear Lord Jesus. I believe that you are the Christ, the son of the living God. You came, showed forth Your love, forgave, lived, died and rose again. I believe You are in heaven today. I need your forgiveness and your LOVE in my own life. Please come into my heart today. Be my Savior and friend for all eternity. I want you to be Lord of All.

Amen.

If you prayed that prayer, put your name and date here,
so you can always point to this time.

Name: ....

Date: ....

Now we invite you to connect with us so
we may help you walk a daily life with Jesus.

Email: cogwe2010@gmail.com

and follow us monthly on our women's web page;

www.wewomenofexcellence.com.

God Bless each of you as we share HIS LOVE with others.

Connect with us with a review at:
Wewomenofexcellence.com

GOD

IS

love

1 John 4:16